Tool Box Kit

Praying Power

Kingdom Principles of Prayer

Dr. Stacy D. Coward, RN, LPC, ThD

UOM, Inc

Tree House Ministries

Tool Box Kit- Praying Power
Kingdom Principles of Prayer

UOM, Inc Tree House Ministry Products are available at special quantity for bulk purchases for the sales and promotions premium fundraiser and educational needs.

For more details write: 3615 Victory Blvd, Ste 105 Portsmouth, Virginia 23704, stacy.coward@yahoo.com (757) 581-3897, Face workbook, UOM, Inc Counseling

Copy right 2021 by UOM, Inc Tree House Ministry Products. This edition published in 2021.

Scripture quotations marked KJV *AMP, NASB* are taken from the King James Version, Amplified Bible, New American Standard Bible (Public Domain)

Compiled and edited by Tree House Ministry.

All rights and reserved to this workbook. No part of this publication can be reproduced, stored in a retrieval system or transmitted in any form by any means –electronic, mechanical. No Photocopying, recording or any other –except brief quotations in printed reviews, without prior written permission of the publisher.

Design by the UOM, Inc Tree House Ministry Products:

ISBN 978-1-716-37548-4 Imprint: Lulu.com

Tool Box Kit- Praying Power
Kingdom Principles of Prayer

THIS BOOK BELONGS TO

_____

Tool Box Kit- Praying Power
Kingdom Principles of Prayer

This book is dedicated to all the people who are trying to figure it out. To the people who need practical tools with real applications that work

This book is written for all those people who are looking for tools to empower them on their success journey.

Everyone seems to have all the quick fix answers but the truth is it takes work and lots of it. Every day we have to work on being the best person we can before that day. This book will show you what to do and what tools you can use to gain success for your life.

Tool Box Kit- Praying Power
Kingdom Principles of Prayer

Contents

Introduction
What is prayer?
What happens when I pray?
What is the purpose of prayer?
Why do I need prayer?
How do I pray with purpose?
Where should I pray?
Should I meditate?
How long should I pray?
How often should I pray?
What should I have in prayer?
When should I pray?
How to avoid praying amiss?
How to align my prayers with God's plan?
What types of prayers are there?
How do I pray?
Foundational pillars

Tool Box Kit- Praying Power
Kingdom Principles of Prayer

Introduction

Prayer is one of the greatest forms of worship. It is a time when we are able to become completely present with God. It can be use in so many ways that will make your life clear and concise. God has blessed us with a way of being able to get a hold of Him at anytime about anything. Prayer is one of the greatest tools a person can ever have to be truly successful in life. I pray that this book is simple enough for a child to understand yet compelling enough to impact a nation. My prayer is that you would grow into everything that God has called you to become and you use the tool of prayer to gain a greater relationship with God our Father.

Tool Box Kit- Praying Power
Kingdom Principles of Prayer

What is prayer?

Prayer is the most powerful tool you have to change your mind set and your reality.

What happens when I pray?

Angels are supernaturally dispatched on your behalf to partner with you to accomplish the will of God. Angels are given specific assignments to assist you, encourage you, protect you, lead and guide you into the path of righteousness for His namesake. Your prayers are written down, discussed and a strategic plan is developed to help you through a providential plan.

What is the purpose of prayer?

Prayer is the tool that we used to talk with God. Prayer helps usher us into the presence of the Holy Spirit. We use prayer to take us to God's throne. The whole purpose of prayer is to get into the presence of the Holy Spirit. Prayer is a form of worship. When we are praying we should continue in prayer until we feel a sense of God's presence. Once we sense God's presence it's time to listen. Many times people spend too much time talking and not listening.

Tool Box Kit- Praying Power
Kingdom Principles of Prayer

Why do I need prayer?

Prayer allows you to supernaturally superimpose the current reality and enter into spiritual portals that shift you into the reality that God sees you.

How do I pray with a purpose?

Spend time with a specific idea. You can start by creating a master list that you will use to pray from daily. Come up with 365 things that you want to spend time talking to God about. Use a daily prayer list that you will work from in order to have a focus on what you are praying about.

Finish out in the Lord's Prayer specifically connecting it to the specific thing you are praying on

Where should I pray?

You can pray anywhere but praying in private places yields the best reward.

Should I meditate in prayer?

Quiet time in prayer is essential. It is important to learn how to quiet your thoughts. Use deep breathing exercises and techniques to focus and clear your thoughts in order to stop your mind from wandering. After you have quieted your thoughts listen for God to give you the instructions for the day

How long should I pray?

You need about thirty minutes to listen to God after you have petitioned Him for your needs He needs to speak to you and give you direction on what to do.

How often should I pray?

The Word of God says pray without ceasing. We should consider prayer an opportunity to change our lives. Therefore we should move with a purpose when it comes to praying. Every opportunity to pray for yourself or other people is as an opportunity for God to begin finishing work in you or someone else. Use your time in prayer to move with a particular purpose in mind.

What should I have in prayer?

Always be prepared to get an answer to your prayer. This means that you stop talking and start listening for God to give you instruction and write the instructions down. Always keep a paper and pencil handy because God always has something to say about your life. God has a vested interest you and He wants to give you instruction every day

Tool Box Kit- Praying Power
Kingdom Principles of Prayer

When should I pray?

Remember this is the day the Lord has made. He made this day for you. You did not create this day. The Lord has made it. Your job is to find out what He is doing today and become a part of the plan of the day. You can be glad in it because you know that whatever happens today is to establish His purpose.

How do I avoid praying Amiss?

Stop praying about the same stuff every day. Pray about what you need God to do with you and for you.

How do I align my prayers with God's Plans?

You are a tool that God should be able to use at His disposal. The Word of God tells us to seek you first the kingdom of God in all of his righteousness and all of these things will be added to you. As you pray believe that if you make God's plans your plans everything else you need will come.

Tool Box Kit- Praying Power
Kingdom Principles of Prayer

What types of prayer are there?

There are many kinds of prayer that work. Here a just a few types of prayers

Thanksgiving prayer
Repentance prayer
Salvation prayer
Healing prayer
Warfare Prayer
A.C.T.S (adore, confess, thank, supplication)
Intercessory Prayer
Corporate Prayer
Fasting and Prayer

All of which create a different kind of momentum in the spirit and natural realm.

How do I pray?

When Jesus was with the disciples this is how He taught them to pray

The Lord's Prayer is the framework for your prayers

Matthew 6:9-13 (King James Version)

9. After this manner therefore pray ye: Our Father which art in heaven, Hallowed be thy name.

10. Thy kingdom come, Thy will be done in earth, as it is in

Tool Box Kit- Praying Power
Kingdom Principles of Prayer

heaven.

11. Give us this day our daily bread.

12. And forgive us our debts, as we forgive our debtors.

13. And lead us not into temptation, but deliver us from evil: For thine is the kingdom, and the power, and the glory, forever. Amen.

Tool Box Kit- Praying Power
Kingdom Principles of Prayer

Foundational Pillar One

Our Father which art in heaven hallow it be thy name thy kingdom come thy will be done on earth as it is in heaven

LORD let your will be done on earth regarding my

1. Husband/ Wife/ family/ children/ grandparents/ parents
2. Job/Business
3. Home/community
4. Health/wealth/resources
5. Relationships/personal and business
6. Transportation
7. Opportunities for growth
8. Challenges from people, situations, circumstances
9. Spiritual growth
10. Education/wisdom/knowledge
11. Taking on new responsibilities
12. Getting the right mentor
13. Mentoring the right people
14. Spending the right time with the right people
15. Working on the right projects at the right time
16. Spending your money on the right things
17. Activating my faith
18. The city officials/teachers
19. The president/nation

Tool Box Kit- Praying Power
Kingdom Principles of Prayer

Foundational Pillar Two

Give us this day our daily bread.

Ask God for what you need TODAY

There is enough food, money, time, energy, love, provision for the day in today.

As you are thinking and praying stop and take time to really think about what you need TODAY.

What would you like to accomplish today?

Ask the Lord to bless your task list for the day which means you must establish a list of things you want to accomplish today.

Manna from Heaven – Provision for the day. Do not waste your time and energy in places that you have not assigned as a priority for today. People will bring you stuff all day long. That is not your assignment so do not take it on. You have prayed and centered your day. Establish your household. That's' their stuff not yours. You have asked for the bread you need for yourself and your family. You did not collect enough manna for their drama. Tell them to go get their bread for the day!

Tool Box Kit- Praying Power
Kingdom Principles of Prayer

Foundational Pillar Three

And forgive us our debts, as we forgive our debtors.

You want God to have mercy and grace on your life.

You want God to forgive you of your mess. But you don't want to be held accountable for the lie you told yesterday or the thought you thought an hour ago. You may not be living in sin so to speak but you definitely have some dirt that you need God to forgive you on. We have too many things that occur on a daily, hourly basis that we need to be able to stand clean before God. I want God to be able to establish the works of my hands so my heart has been clean toward Him and the people. It is not all about my outward sin. It is the inner man for most people that needs a daily cleansing and forgiveness.

Not trusting in the Lord is sin

Not telling the whole truth is sin

Not thinking kind thoughts toward others is sin

Being in debt is sin

It's not all the drug addicts, prostitutes and thieves that are the sinners! Ouch! Lord I'm still a sinner. I need deliverance from my unbelief in the middle of the storm. I don't trust you enough when I am in the middle of the crisis. By now I should be commanding the storms to stop and the water to turn solid as I walk on it. I do not believe you enough. You have been with me so long and yet I still do not have the level of faith that I need to move my mountains with my mouth. I repent for my level of unbelief. I am too far in the relationship not to believe you for everything that I need. My children being saved filled with the Holy Spirit because Lord you already established in heaven and earth. My finances being in correct alignment with what God is doing. Lord my body needs to be completely healed, pain free, sickness free, healthy and strong. Lord forgive me, I do need forgiveness.

Forgive Others

Hurry up and forgive the people who offend you because when you view your life you aren't not walking in all that holy glory you may think. You need to forgive others because He forgave you. If God can forgive you or your internal messiness then you can certainly forgive those people who publicly did you wrong. At least with them you know that they offended you. Many of the people you have offended you did it in silence and that is even worse because you created a spiritual battle with them and they do not know where it is coming from unless they pray. They do not even know who to protect themselves from. At least the person

Tool Box Kit- Praying Power
Kingdom Principles of Prayer

who offended you let you know they did not like you and they were not on your side. You have the benefit of protecting yourself from them moving forward. So whose sin in greater?

Tool Box Kit- Praying Power
Kingdom Principles of Prayer

Foundational Pillar Five

And lead us not into temptation

Ask the Lord to lead you to a place where YOU will not be tempted to sin.

Jesus was led us to the wilderness and their He was tempted. Lord keep me out the wilderness! Lead me to the promise land! Let all my steps be established to move me towards the promise land and not the wilderness.

Tool Box Kit- Praying Power
Kingdom Principles of Prayer

Foundational Pillar Six

But deliver us from evil:

Deliver me from evil. Pick me up and carry me far away from the foolishness. I do not want to waste my day on anything that is foolish. You can keep your kee- kee kooing laughing about being a part of the foolishness. You can keep your pulling me to the side to talk about people.

Don't let my heart be angry, envious or jealous toward anyone. Do not let my thoughts create hurt, harm or danger towards another person

Tool Box Kit- Praying Power
Kingdom Principles of Prayer

Foundational Pillar Seven

For thine is the kingdom,

Father everything that is going on in this earthly dimension you have given me leadership, ruler ship and authority because it's your kingdom. Father you have full dominion and you have given me power and authority on this earthly dimension. Everything belongs to you and I belong to you. I am adopted into your kingdom as your child and therefore I have the authority to rule in this earthly dimension.

Tool Box Kit- Praying Power
Kingdom Principles of Prayer

Foundational Pillar Eight

And the power,

God you are my power. Lord you are my source. Lord you are my strength. Lord you are my refuge. Lord you are where I recharge my life. Lord you are where I am made whole. Lord with you I am strong.

This is your recognition and acknowledgement that God is the source of all your power, might and strength. It is His spirit that empowers you to do great and mighty works

Tool Box Kit- Praying Power
Kingdom Principles of Prayer

Foundational Pillar Nine

And the glory,

Lord let my heart and my mind all be about glorifying you. Let my actions glorify you. Let my behaviors glorify you. Let my work glorify you. Let my thoughts glorify you. Everything that I do should be glorifying you.

It is easy to shine a light on the goodness of God because He is so good to us. Without Him we are nothing but with Him we can become all He has planned for us.

Tool Box Kit- Praying Power
Kingdom Principles of Prayer

Foundational Pillar Ten

Forever

This work shall be established as irrefutable, everlasting and eternal. It is sealed by the blood of Jesus and written down by angels to carry out the works according to the Word of God.

The Word of God last forever therefore whatever we declare and decree stands the test of time. We are merely awaiting the manifestation of God's promises towards us.

Amen.

SO BE IT

Let it be done

Let it be establish

It is finished

This is the benediction. It is the closing remarks that put a period on the prayer. It says I have finished and I believe that I have established it and it is done already. It says I am in agreement with God and I second the motion.

Tool Box Kit- Praying Power
Kingdom Principles of Prayer

Hopefully this little foundation's of prayer book was enough to shed some light on prayer.

There are many, many ways and forms of prayer. The goal is to connect with God and get an answer for your life's question.

There are no particular rules for prayer. It is about talking to the Father, the judge, the friend, the provider, the protector. When you have something going on in life you need and answer and prayer will get you the answers you need.

I am praying for you and with you!

Love

Dr. Coward

Lightning Source UK Ltd.
Milton Keynes UK
UKHW012026231222
414417UK00004B/9